Life in the ice

T0372053

The Arctic sits at the top
of the world. Sea ice
spreads all around it.

Treeless plains called tundra spread over the land.

The Arctic is freezing.
Storms here are bitter.

4

However, there are ways to make life pleasant in this chilly home.

Seals have a thick layer of blubber.

This heavy layer helps them to keep energy to swim in the chilly seas.

Under this bear's thick white fur is black skin. This soaks up the sun's rays, ready to keep the bear snug.

Slightly webbed paws keep the bear swimming at a steady pace. This helps it to cross the wide sea to find food on sheets of ice.

The Arctic fox has layers of fluffy fur. They are like a thick winter sweater for this small fox.

The threat of a blizzard comes quickly here. The Arctic fox can dig into the snow to hide.

The fox covers up
with its thick tail.

The musk ox digs into the frozen ground to reach food.

The walrus can drop its own pulse. This stops it getting cold so it can stay in the sea longer.

This Arctic whale uses its head to break the ice. This lets it take a breath to dive down deep.

Living things in the Arctic are meant to be in this wilderness. They love life in the ice.

Words to blend

spread	pleasant	heavy
ready	sweater	threat
steady	breath	head
spreads	meant	Arctic
wilderness	tundra	walrus
energy	blizzard	blubber

Before reading

Synopsis: The Arctic is freezing cold. Animals that live there have lots of clever ways to make life pleasant in their chilly home.

Review phonemes and graphemes: /ear/ ere, eer; /air/ are, ear, ere; /j/ ge, dge, g; /s/ c, ce, sc, se, st; /c/ ch; /u/ o, o-e, ou

Focus phoneme: /e/   **Focus grapheme:** ea

Book discussion: Look at the cover, and read the title together. Talk about the Arctic – what do children already know about it? Share their ideas. Ask: *What kind of book do you think this is – fiction or non-fiction? How do you know? What kind of information do you think we will find out about the Arctic?*

Link to prior learning: Remind children that the sound /e/ as in 'pen' can also be spelled 'ea'. Flip through pages 2–7 and challenge children to point out as many words with the /e/ sound as they can find.

Vocabulary check: blubber: fat that sea animals have – 'a thick layer of blubber' means 'a thick layer of fat'.

Decoding practice: Display the words 'steady, 'head', 'breath' and 'heavy'. Can children circle the letter string that makes the /e/ sound, and read each word?

Tricky word practice: Display the word 'are'. Tell children that the whole of this word is tricky! The whole word says /ar/. Practise reading and spelling this word.

After reading

Apply learning: Discuss the book. Ask: *Which animal did you like the most? Why? What was the most interesting fact about Arctic animals for you?*

Comprehension

- What colour is a polar bear under its fur? (black)
- How do seals keep energy? (They have a thick layer of blubber.)
- What does the Arctic fox do when there is a blizzard? (dig into the snow to hide)

Fluency

- Pick a page that most of the group read quite easily. Ask them to reread it with pace and expression. Model how to do this if necessary.
- Challenge children to read pages 8–9 out loud, as if they were a TV presenter.
- Practise reading the words on page 17.

Tricky words review

the	of	are
have	into	once
many	ask	because
who	two	whole
friend	water	their